HEREDITY AND OTHER INVENTIONS

Poems

Sharona Muir

C&R Press
Conscious & Responsible

Winter Soup Bowl Chapbook 2017
Second Collection
1 of 2 CB6

Printed in the United States of America

First Edition
1 2 3 4 5 6 7 8 9

Cover Design by Sally Underwood
Interior Design by Ali Chica

Library of Congress Cataloging-in-Publication Data

ISBN: 978-1-936196-80-7

C&R Press
Conscious & Responsible
www.crpress.org

For special discounted bulk purchases please contact:
C&R Press sales@crpress.org

Thank you to our generous Patreon patrons.

For my mother and fellow poet, Marilyn Bentov, with love

HEREDITY AND OTHER INVENTIONS

TABLE OF CONTENTS

The Arrival Gate

Your life ended one minute after takeoff.
A flaw branched through an engine casing,
and shapeless clouds engulfed
the last seconds you had of yourself.

In free fall, souls slip from brows
like daydreams. Bodies are gently sloughed
in free fall, at higher altitudes,
but not at the takeoff, with its moaning boost and tilted rows:

stressed metal octaves
sang through pillow-wadded skulls.
Ice rattled in clear cups
abandoned by so many startled hands, at once

everywhere, clinging. Listen! This song's
lines are your instructions. Here
is the red-lined exit, wide as the mouth
of a soprano, prolonging, through the awed hall,

a miracle.
Out of orange body bags the exploded jet's passengers
rise, smoke faces becoming flesh;
their personal belongings reattach
handles and shoulder-straps to hands and shoulders;

the crowd surges slowly up the jetway,
spilling into the arrival bay. Monitors show ARRIVED.
We walk the human corridors. You have not changed.
You have not changed, and I ask why you died.

After the Persian

Here is a tawny doe who chews a reed's tip;
behind the reeds, a lion whose red tongue droops.

Yet in the doe's prayer, the lion is a singing bird,
and in the lion's prayer, the doe is a flowering tree.

And in the bird's prayer, the tree that blooms
incarnadine and evergreen, is our mother Eve

in whose breasts the Milky Way wakes to our cries,
and in whose arms our fallen cities die.

My Father's Laser

A black pond holding a white moon
holds no more still than this winter
night. The laboratory door shuts:
we stand on the driveway gravel.
Such is the cold that vacuum splinters
to stars: we find a father, beside one
little five-pointed girl. A traveled
moon continues to burn white-hot
fifty years ago. I hold the laser
like a boxed wine, molded in steel,
while he speaks, whose bass croon
enconches in the ear. Like an ember
glowing, as I press the button,
a dot reddens on the clapboard wall,
a bead drawn on my father's house.
It is coherent light. It is purpose,
the even heartbeat. I send its beam
dancing invisibly on the gray marb_ed
surface of the moon: I remember
imagining the dead, cratered dust
turr_ed faint rubies in one thought.
This strange world was my dream
inherited from him. The inventor
is dead, forty years come winter,
and fifty years ago, I held t_e laser.
Our white breaths mingled and hung

The Tank and The Fossil

The tank hatch shuts

Forty-eight hours
to go inside   His body armor baulky   His
headset jabbers   Voices like frying circuits
Orange data scrolling in the computer screen
He calculates and reports   Gets jolted sideways
Wallslammed   Fortunate because he's far
to the rear of the combat   Lobbing high
shells that target enemy infantry   But
if their rockets falling behind our lines hit this tank
He does not know day or night   The time is If

He climbs out and it's night   Desert darkness

Naked he sleeps   Naked he wakes covered in mist
His hand does not find his glasses   Picks up
a small snail of sandstone
flecked with dewy quartz   A million years
His palm looks young
This morning's getting light

Theodorakis' Ballad*

"You've been told lies. Now sing the real words,"
Theodorakis growls from center stage.
Inside your ear's the hammer of this world.

From his throat, the notes are husky chords;
a black-browed Greek, iron with age,
who's been told lies, now sings the real words:

the ballad of Mauthausen that he forged
out of a girl's hand, a simple image.
Inside your ear, the hammer works her world.

You're a thousand-headed audience, stirred
to dead quiet. He holds the floodlit stage.
You, lied to, never sang the real words

the way he does, raising his palm upward.
A girl's cold hand releases rage
far inside. Your ear's hammer hums. The world

beaten into a sword
has served obedient in every age
you've been told lies. Now, sing the real words.
Inside your ear's the hammer of this world.

* This poem is based on Mikis Theodorakis' performance of his famous
song, "Mauthausen."

9

Clouds Over Jerusalem, In Winter

As if they were trying to build on a different thought
the clouds accumulate between sun and the city,
so the beams go wide and break into sheaves of light.
It is as if the clouds were trying to reflect the city

without interference of what makes objects and colors
hard and sharp. From the washed, pale stone they are the breath
between our words, and the sound of Shiloah running underground
released to the upper air, so soft, so limitless.

They are like the explosion between a woman and her lover,
spears, fountains, pregnancies of air, sleep's furrows,
changing without changing their nature,
and one bedsheet rumpling on a line is like a child to them.

They are the builders who would take us up in their arms,
but they have built only a Jerusalem of thoughts.
From the sides of the clouds bloom our epic episodes,
bloodless. Bloodless.

The Recoilless Cannon

-- Haifa, 1995

Nature devised me for remembering.
I am escorted to this secret Ministry
of Defense Museum, illumined room

where six slim missiles finned with X
are ranged, war by war, on wheeled frames,
and share one striking angle

as though hypnotized. I half-kneel,
and rap the russet iron barrel
of a cannon. "You father never told you?"

asks the unnameable curator. "All his life
he never told me." The old voice descends,
embarrassed, "Some need to forget

We found this cannon in a weedy field."
I feel inside the hollow bore as smooth as
five feet of river water. It lacks

that spiral groove through which the shell flies
spinning out – like death's
negative DNA –

so I, whose DNA is bound
up with the state's defense,
discover my father's cannon was a water-pipe

until its end, shaped like a flowerpot,
was welded shut, then pierced with apertures
like cruel smiles.

I have learned how in 1948
the darkening sea pounded underneath

the sun's dazzling-down. Like a pendulum

strung above tramped sand, a cannon hung.
Generals watched gravely. The Old Man's
clenched face reflected off their brows.

Then, Father, you released
the forward thunder – the backward blast
blew a stopwatch from your palm –

but the rope and the suspended barrel forgot
to move. Waves turned maroon,
while only the city in its electric haze

trembled a little … ("You really understand,"
says the curator. I nod in my flowery
postwar synthetics.) Action has no reaction,

pretends the recoilless cannon. If recoil
is nature's memory of a shot,
then you devised this weapon to forget.

I touch ten azimuth adjustment holes;
covet, on its short chain, the key
belonging to the middle-aged state.

Are you only memory? The change in the air
to enchantment when you laughed,
your lighter-than-fire atmosphere –

somewhere you must be passing seventy,
the compass clipped to the dashboard
a small well prisoning the star of will

that all inventions have in common. Wind
glitters across the windshield,
stung by time's dust, and you're singing

in what was your only tongue for singing;
your eyes, though, are nettled red,

shadows compress your olive cheeks;
your voice scrapes high notes – notes I
inherited like a personal frequency:
I sing to know and not to know what is,

I make believe the dead are listening. And some
leave their truth in a weedy field.

You ask, Curator, am I proud?

Say that, as truth with fact,
My DNA is bound up with the state.
I touch bolts steadfast for half a century

because this bastard sister will outlast me,
passing no judgment on fragile hands;
this iron mouth calling for water and fire.

Winter in Jerusalem

When, through an open door,
I saw white tiles turning rose,
a small fire in its foil-bright stove,
and heard the paraffin wick cough,

and smelled the air drugged with inedible honey,
I realized that I'd been humming
my father's favorite melody.
Then it was hard to go on walking

down the Street of the Chain,
its cobblestones all cratered with water,
and under them, waters of the cisterns
like the past deep under memory.

At the reed mat, squashed in rain,
I left my shoes, and entered Omar's Shrine.
Around the dome, a frieze of fire
circled in gold sleeves, as tractable as pain.

The eye of the spire was dazzling,
and the rugs smelled of exhausted feet
as if a crowd sheltered here,
but only one Arab was singing verses

in a voice clearer than any fire,
rising more steadily than the rain fell,
as if he drew his breath out of the verse itself.
He was singing of the night journey

from hot Mecca to cold Jerusalem.
I pondered the dark altar stone
where Abraham had bound a son
as his song raised his Prophet into heaven.

Nocturne for the Treaty Signing

Jerusalem 1993

How long my hands
have been well-worn
thoughts of an automatic rifle.

Ajar,
my wrought-iron gate.
A mulberry tree, in leaf,
is shadowing the courtyard
tiles; the back of my hand
pouring wine's
caught in a dark pattern.

The walled Old City stares
across the valley, all luminous stone
like a white pomegranate
packed with ripe tears.
Life's brief,
hatred is fine
to abandon;

my garden quietly fills
with opening bars of music
broadcast from Jerusalem: the news.

In My Father's Laboratory

*A new steerable angiography catheter ... will soon take much
of the hazard out of hospital procedure ...*
Product Engineering, 1969

For this device, someone had to die
who had no restrictions on his heart
being cast in acrylic. Clear as a bubble,
like the blood-pump of an angel stilled,
it rests on the workbench stained
with acids and quick-set resins.

A child can work this instrument. I hold
the catheter's brass cone, thumb the joystick
and a dark wire writhes into the ventricle,
inquiring, left and right, where is the clot?
"We'll inject photo-optic fluid into the veins,"
my father boasts. "People will be saved."

They will shine from within, like human daylight,
their hope the only worm in them.

Canzone: Meteor Elegy

A star flees space
lightly, in the time
a spark glows in a startled space
it leaves dark. With escape-
trailing glimmer, a free light
dishevels the starred spaces ...
Einstein measured space
by point of view.   My mind's
doubled over my mind's
wound, a hidden space;
my words are wasted
measuring their waste.

American flight 191 heading west
sheared blue space
that thundered black – his last word was
unknowable – the crash blasted wasteland
a mile wide. Since that time,
through all his wasted
future, my father lives, as far stars waste
away to starlight,
he is daily light.
The hourglass waist,
the stem of falling sand. Love's a determined
loser at the game it masterminds.

The irony of a divided mind
is lively, but on life irony's wasted . .
Czech gene-strands are mine
like strung crystal, reminders
of darkness. A dark and hidden space
of maternal earth minds
our lost family.   He kept his mind
a wound never mended in time
to die whole. He fled time
and again into fast planes, reminded
of what made him go lightly –

he still travels light.

Through a library skylight
(dark, rain-scoured, unmindful
of absent gazes) a hollow light
castle manifests, alight
with pure watts
of yearning. The knife-lit
turrets, a hawk delighting,
the crescent spaces
bridges span, the scarp-walled space
lightning
dazzles in transfixed: Time
branching all at one time.

What captures my father? Wartime
bivouacs, tents ruffled with light
hot wind.   An English grammar and the Times.
Years when military time
was natural rhythm, planting mines
his utmost skill. He had the time
of his life. A cigarette to pass the slow burn time
of the cordite charge that was
his testament to each golden wasteful
African dawn … He checks the time:
now. Gray mountains space
apart the stars. He feels sound collapse

and hugs ground. Stars avalanche through space.
The flash, timed,
passes over, plumed light.
He's running, never minding
how all around him dreams the sandy waste.

The Most Unsafe Market in Jerusalem

Each moment some turquoise iron door in a white wall or a carpenter
whose hands in rough canvas gloves, settling a plank on a bench,
make your spine feel massaged, or sacks of walnuts beside sacks of
pecans, or white peaches, green peaches, hairy peaches, cherries,
lemons, melons, two lanes of people, parsley, loquats, pita and sesame
and poppy breads and sweet cakes, figs and dates, candies and halvah
wheels, green onions, flat silver fish and flat straw-yellow fish with
gold irises, sausages, nightgowns, chickens, God, what isn't there?
Grocers hollering, *Three shekels the kilo, the government's fallen,*
three shekels, apricots, the government's fallen! – which is

a metaphor for now.

At My Age, Like Me

At my age, like me, my father's divorced.
But he is more Israeli: his drab shirt
mapping sweat as the telephone warms
with a crony and a product and a deal,

its wrapped cord snaking across a verbal
cactus garden, where he stalks, or stoops
to pick up the child's leftover rusk,
nibble its toothmarked cream cheese.

Meanwhile, placed on mental hold,
his other room emits rhythmic shrieks,
thrillings of springs. His three-year-old
jumps and jumps on the wry, unmade bed

almost, in thin air, gaining happiness,
a separate dimension where children fly.

Heredity

Stanford University, 1988

Adam and Eve, at the first
Human Genome Conference
separated onstage. Footlights
glazed the trellised ivy
flanking their black platform;
the backdrop, a movie screen
on which Adam projected slides.

Stage left: his pinkish cannonball
bespectacled, his magisterial
spiel squealing with feedback,
his reflective papers
on the halogen-lit lectern.

Stage right: Eve, revealed in full
dress, an inflight stewardess
charmingly miming safety
procedures - she interpreted
for the deaf. Groomed leaves
brushed her neutral calves.

Adam displayed a chromosome,
squiggling with the future
endowments of drosophila,
and he named some genes
Unlike the fruit-fly's, human
genetic material's details
are infinitely difficult of access.
(The hushed hall relished
our secret gifts.) Next slide.
Here is our problem: (a caricature
of melted structural girders.
An ICBM-black arrow slid
around, smoothly panicked.
No, no.) A signless roadmap
of continental interstates. The X'ed

California town was where
Adam lost his wallet. *Imagine*
him retracing his footsteps
from Massachusetts, searching
I-90 for that wallet: one human gene.

Squinting at what Adam lost
as futilely as doomed
balloons bob along a ceiling,
the auditorium of heads
nodded. Translating Adam,
Eve's quick gestures loosed
filaments of immediate past.
Her hands loomed air
to patterned gossamer,
fabricating space and time,
and the material identical
to both, impassioned dream;
as I search my mirrored eyes
to see again my father's
clear thread doubling back,
an emerging figure. Adam,
the translation ran, was lost.
He stole along dark roads.
I had no questions afterwards,
when screen, lectern, plants,
Adam, Eve, and descendants
left not a rack behind.

But I had forever lost,
now remembering to regret,
the small scab, like flaked gold,
my father stored in a cottonball
among his eyeglass screws
and watchsprings, till he died:
the snipped cord of my birth --
my question is why my loose
end ended in those clear cells:
his miniature plastic drawers
where circuit chips, resistors,
left- and right-threaded screws

like sutras, readied to connect
his laboratory's microcosm?

What did the inventor make
of fatherhood?

Like a marvelous griffon,
he bent his tufted brows,
and his eyelids, over a gleam,
tightened at their corners;
one hand wrote, the other beat
a tattoo upon an inch of air.
His notebook, brown as horn,
opened to fine ballpoint
illuminated mechanisms
his script flew past. Behind,
one thousand reagent bott_es
shelved the laboratory walls
opposite continuous windows
filled with thin birches'
interlaced frost, or green light.

Machines freighted worktables:
smooth serpentining cables
choked the outlets; alligator
clips' petty jaws bit sparks;
a transformer uttered a bass
twangle, ignored by monitors.
A stylus traced the world's
teeth on spooling tape. Where
a bench sweated solder, the small
plastic chest pearled it over
wracked scrap-metal. I. Ben-Tov
Devised what he lived from daily,
ranging around this jumble,
singing, to the pegboard wall's
hand power tools, heraldic Black
& Decker, charged with orange,
each sawblade a chrome shudder.
Lathe and sander stood on trestles,
while metaphysical engines

hovered just beyond reach,
turning ideas out of nothing.
Telephones jarred; a receiver rode
his shoulder like a bold crow.
He stooped over his lathe's
hum, scream and steel shavings'
geranium odor (oh my bright
childish fistfuls!). He broke off
singing, and raised a silk-
finished component to the light.

When death froze the nerve
of his laboratory, and blacked
the clear windows, not knowing
where to look among the self-
absorbed objects, I sat down
and powered the oscilloscope.
A blip raced. A green line
rose and fell like wavy rope,
caracoled like coiling vines
or helical DNA; a spell wound
around time's wound. Hurt
to be enthralled, I looked
outside. Birches in beckoning leaf.

A shunting of the frame, some
shift of genetic code-triplets,
warp-strands raised or lowered,
and the shuttle, holy boat, shot
laced birches or a woman
through the web that animates
its loom.   All daughterhood
or fatherhood meant was thrall
to the fabrication of our parts.
Yet, discovering whom I lost --
that loose end of my being
he treasured as if for use --
I dreamed heredity was love.

The Psalm of the Shutters

Slit
zinc shutters,
hot as armor,
radiate
ten white
lines on the dim walls, write
a prayer
so exact
it is light; the opened shutters sway
wide,
ordinary
hours trek
out like fighters,
and back.

Oh citadel
rotten with sun!

Jerusalem awaits
the tranced afternoon
that ambers each
tree branch or glass pane, within reach,
the brown children scattering a fountain
that juggles, winks, and lives
under a spell,
out of dust a yellow-crested hoopoe's dive
toward mountains
folded in haze.

What is not lost gives
rise to soft praise.

The Gate of Babylon

The Berlin Museum's halls echo more footfalls
than there are visitors.

             In a skylit room
stands an arch, glazed brick,
of such dimensions that tandem horsemen
can trot through, not lowering their spears:
the Ishtar Gate.

             How far from Babylon's
brown canals where oarstrokes furrowed
indigo images of walls,
and bronze towers, by palmy steps, zigzagged
                   to paradise;
how far from home.

             The sight of her,
steadying the three-days-distant caravan
gradually disappeared;

             turned into mound,
trenched excavation, Prussian monument,
cargo aboard an armored train to Moscow;
metamorphosed into this postwar exhibit

             where the entrance
to the dead Imperium's reassembled:
blistered lapis wall and giant frieze
of fabulous animals, Babylon's memories.

             Her ancient menagerie
silently paces the restored facade.
The pale bull has eyes alive with kohl,

one indigo tier lower, the serpent
struts, despite Eden, on eagle's claws,
the snarling lion treads a bottom row
of cream rosettes, his ochre muscles
deforming the bricks.

Clouds pass

and the gallery's dim. Visitors adjust
their headphones' multilingual muffs,
like cold children,
                        awaiting sacrifice.

Shelter from Thunderstorms

Cold, drenched, in your bones a clamor
percussive as the rain, you knock
at his dark door. It opens, look,

the windows shine, and windows within windows
shine; a spectrum glows upright
on bookshelves packed tight. The historian knew
you'd appear (you all do.) As for the hand
he won't extend – it's understandable,
his handiwork must recompose the dead
in their dirt library, on their night table ...

and though you've known a similar place, you're here
keeping step with your shadow: a dance for two.

And when he speaks, the words bear, reverberant,
the human truth you survived so it might answer you.

Breath Diviner

Leaves breathe. What leaves,
breathes. I lie
beside you
in this dim room
with four all-knowing windows:

from them, the moon
leans
onto your long pillow
as I see your breath rise,
subside.

Love,
the lemniscate's
two leaves
are not you and I
whose sighs are numbered.

But in our garden
grow, near-infinite,
the swimming treetops
of a minor sky.

And better, too,
than all the voluminous leaves
dictated when the god
 – brute knowledge --
seized the sibyl's

throat-strings:
vaginal outcries,
the future's awful
schedule …

The shape of a deer's
ear, outline of her
vulnerable eye

watches above
a fawn all summer long.

In caresses let us be
shadily forgetful,
loose-leaved.

Can we, in our
nostrils' crossing breaths --
sweet interference! –
know even breathing
to its depths?

At ocean-bottom
a diver's lungs shrink
to lemon-size,
and air's an ocean.

Breathe as deep
as you can, oh breathe,
diver,
the lemon-tree in flower.

I give you leave.

Wristwatch on a Nightstand

When sparrows shrill like thawing ice
and framed panes lighten in the room,
the man turns underneath the bedclothes,
links my fingers to his, and to the scar
where a caress slides faster up his thumb.
Breathing in rhythm's a kind of silence;
a sheet meanders weightless to the floor
his bare leg droops over, knee-deep in sun.
The seconds fall asleep. He's all raised hope,
I am all his hope needs to be embraced,
and the morning exerts its clearest rays
to lift a cry after the scattered birds;
and if, below their wings, time must be kept,
Paradise is the time our bodies keep.

After Orpheus

Against death, I became a child
perched on a moldered step,
and saw my father's laboratory
revive its chittering machines;

again, tiles fluoresced like cells
in the cement basement ceiling;
his white coat hung on a chair,
slide-rule sulking in one pocket.

I sang a threshold in midair,
a tall frame and a starry keyhole;
it was no reasoned hypothesis
following close behind my shoulder;

but, holding any door for him,
I had that trick of looking back.

Acknowledgments

"Clouds Over Jerusalem," in The Paris Review

"The Psalm of the Shutters," and "Wristwatch on a Nightstand,"
in Partisan Review

"Shelter from Thunderstorms,
in Stand

"The Recoilless Cannon," and "Heredity,"
in Michigan Quarterly Review

"Meteor Elegy," and "The Arrival Gate"
in Missouri Review

"My Father's Laser," "In My Father's Laboratory,"
and "After Orpheus,"
in Denver Quarterly

"Nocturne for the Treaty Signing," and "After the Persian,"
in Ploughshares

"Theodorakis' Ballad,"
and "The Tank and the Fossil,"
in Virginia Quarterly Review

"Winter in Jerusalem,"
in Prairie Schooner

"The Most Unsafe Market in Jerusalem,"
in Agni Review, online

"Breath Diviner"
in Signs of Life: Contemporary Jewelry Art and Literature, Facere Gallery, 2011

C&R PRESS CHAPBOOKS

C&R Press hosts two chapbook selection periods from June to September and November to March coupled with a reading in New York City each year. The Winter Soup Bowl and Summer Tide Pool Chapbook Series are open to new and established writers in poetry, fiction, essay and other creative writing.

2017 WINTER SOUP BOWL SELECTIONS

Heredity and Other Inventions
by Sharona Muir

On Innacuracy
by Joe Manning

2016 Summer Tide Pool

Cuntstruck
by Kate Northrop

Relief Map
by Erin M. Bertram

Love Undefined
by Jonathan Katz

2016 Winter Soup Bowl

Notes from the Negro Side of the Moon
by Earl Braggs

A Hunger Called Music: A Verse History in Black Music
by Meredith Nnoka

OTHER C&R PRESS TITLES

FICTION

Ivy vs. Dogg
by Brian Leung

A History of the Cat In Nine Chapters or Less
by Anis Shivani

While You Were Gone
by Sybil Baker

Spectrum
by Martin Ott

That Man in Our Lives
by Xu Xi

SHORT FICTION

Meditations on the Mother Tongue
by An Tran

The Protester Has Been Released
by Janet Sarbanes

ESSAY AND CREATIVE NONFICTION

Immigration Essays
by Sybil Baker

Je suis l'autre: Essays and Interrogations
by Kristina Marie Darling

Death of Art
by Chris Campanioni

POETRY

Negro Side of the Moon
by Early Braggs

Holdfast
by Christian Anton Gerard

Ex Domestica
by E.G. Cunningham

Collected Lies and Love Poems
by John Reed

Imagine Not Drowning
by Kelli Allen

Les Fauves
by Barbara Crooker

Tall as You are Tall Between Them
by Annie Christain

The Couple Who Fell to Earth
by Michelle Bitting

CHAPBOOKS

On Innacuracy by Joe Manning
Cuntstruck by Kate Northrop
Relief Map by Erin Bertram
Love Undefined by Jonathan Katz
Ugly Love: Notes from the Negro Side of the Moon by Earl Braggs
A Hunger Called Music: A Verse History in Black Music
by Meredith Nnoka

www.ingramcontent.com/pod-product-compliance
Lightning Source LLC
Chambersburg PA
CBHW032007060426
42449CB00032B/1204